SCHIRMER'S LIBRARY
OF MUSICAL CLASSICS

Vol. 2131

SELECTED PIANO MASTERPIECES

EARLY ADVANCED LEVEL

16 Pieces by 10 Composers

ISBN 978-1-4950-8803-2

G. SCHIRMER, Inc.

DISTRIBUTED BY

www.schirmer.com
www.halleonard.com

CONTENTS

Allegro barbaro

Tempo giusto ($\bullet$ = 76 – 84)

Béla Bartók

Adagio cantabile

from Piano Sonata in C minor, "Pathétique"

Ludwig van Beethoven
Op. 13

a) To the best of our knowledge no one has yet remarked the striking affinity of the theme of this movement, even with reference to its external melodic structure, to that of one of the loftiest *Adagios* of grandest scope from the Master's last period; — we mean the *Adagio* of the Ninth Symphony, written almost a quarter of a century later. The performance of both demands an equally inspired mood. The player's task, to "make his fingers sing," may perhaps necessitate a more frequent use of the pedal than we have indicated, which must of course be controlled by a most watchful ear.

b) This first middle section of the Rondo (for such this *Adagio* is in form) may be taken slightly *meno andante*, i. e., slower; but no more so than needful (so as not to drag), and, therefore, in only a few places.

c) The turns in this and the next measure should not commence with, but immediately after, a sixteenth-note in the bass, thus: and:

a) A tasteful execution of this grace is impossible in strict time. An abbreviation of the first two principal notes (C and B♭) being quite as impracticable as a shifting of the inverted mordent into the preceding measure as an unaccented appoggiatura, the measure must simply be extended by an additional 32nd-note.

b) In this repetition of the theme, the left hand may be allowed to play a more expressive part; and, on the whole, a somewhat lighter shading of the melody is now admissible by way of contrast to the following (gloomier) middle section.

c) The ascending diminished fifth may be phrased, as it were, like a question, to which the succeeding bass figure may be regarded as the answer.

a) It appears advisable slightly to hasten this measure and the next, and then to retard the third not inconsiderably; the former on account of the cessation in the harmonic advance, the latter by reason of the varied modulation, which must be quite free from disquieting haste in its return to the theme.

b) Though strictly subordinated to the melody, the triplets should be brought out with animated distinctness.

c) The two 32nd-notes in the melody may very properly be sounded with the last note of the triplet of 16th-notes in the accompaniment; whereas a mathematically exact division would probably confuse both parts.

a) Execute like a triplet:

b) In the original, the shading of this passage is marked differently from that two measures before, the *dimi-nuendo* already beginning with C, and not with A♭ as here marked. This latter nuance – the prolongation of the *crescendo* – appeals to our feeling as the more delicate, "more tenderly passionate," to quote Richard Wagner's happy remark on the "Interpretation of Beethoven."

c) Mark the separation of the slurs in this figure and those following; the six notes sound trivial if slurred together.

Adagio sostenuto

from Piano Sonata in C-sharp minor, "Moonlight"

Ludwig van Beethoven
Op. 27, No. 2

Abbreviations: M. T. signifies Main Theme; S. T., Sub-Theme; Cl. T., Closing Theme; D. G., Development-group; R., Return; Tr., Transition; Md. T., Mid-Theme; Ep., Episode.

a) It is evident that the highest part, as the melody, requires a firmer touch than the accompanying triplet-figure; and the first note in the latter must never produce the effect of a doubling of the melody in the lower octave.

b) A more frequent use of the pedal than is marked by the editor, and limited here to the most essential passages, is allowable; it is not advisable, however, to take the original directions *sempre senza sordini* (i. e., without dampers) too literally.

15

a) The player must guard against carrying his hand back with over-anxious haste. For, in any event, a strict pedantic observance of time is out of place in this period, which has rather the character of an improvisation.

a) The notes with a dash above them may properly be dwelt upon in such a way as to give them the effect of suspensions, e. g., : in fact, a utilization of the inner parts, in accordance with the laws of euphony and the course of the modulation, is recommended throughout the piece.

Rhapsody
in G minor

Johannes Brahms
Op. 79, No. 2

Intermezzo
in A Major
from *Six Pieces for Piano*

Johannes Brahms
Op. 118, No. 2

Fantaisie-Impromptu
in C-sharp minor

Frédéric Chopin
Op. 66 (Posthumous)

Tempo I° (Allegro agitato)

Klindworth:

à Madame Camilla Pleyel

Nocturne
in E-flat Major

Frédéric Chopin
Op. 9, No. 2

à Madame la Comtesse Delphine Potocka

Waltz

in D-flat Major
"Minute"

Frédéric Chopin
Op. 64, No. 1

Molto vivace

Clair de lune

from *Suite bergamasque*

Claude Debussy

Tempo I

ppp

Arabesque No. 2
from *Two Arabesques*

Claude Debussy

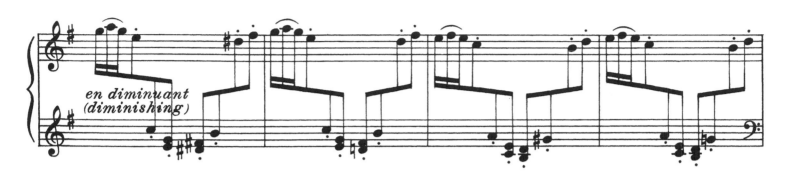

La cathédrale engloutie

from *Préludes*, Book 1

Claude Debussy

Profondément calme (Dans une brume doucement sonore)

*) **Doux et fluide**

*)

*) Debussy, in his piano-roll recording (Welte-Mignon), played measures 7–12 and 22–83 in double speed.

Peu à peu sortant de la brume

sempre pp

p marqué pp

p marqué pp

p

marqué

Augmentez progressivement (Sans presser)

f

più f

Sonore sans dureté

sff

ff

Un peu moins lent (Dans une expression allant grandissant)

Wedding Day at Troldhaugen

from *Lyric Pieces*

Edvard Grieg
Op. 65, No. 6

Liebestraum No. 3
from *Three Liebesträume: Three Notturnos*

Franz Liszt

Più animato, con passione

Prelude
in G minor

Sergei Rachmaninoff
Op. 23, No. 5

Alla marcia (♩=108)

Un poco meno mosso

poco a poco accelerando e cresc. al Tempo I

Prelude
in A minor

Alexander Scriabin
Op. 11, No. 2

Allegretto ♩ = 138

Warum?
(Why?)
from *Fantasiestücke*

Robert Schumann
Op. 12, No. 3